Commendations

"Deciding how to 'live out you[r]
of work is one of the most impo[rtant]
Christian can make. This book i[s]
practical advice for those who a[re]
the 24/7 life."

Jill Garrett, Consultant

"Once again Matt Bird tackles an issue that we have all
shied away from for far too long. His book is practical,
insightful and helpful for anyone trying to become
a round peg in a round hole in the world of work. I
thoroughly recommend it."

Gary Streeter, MP for South West Devon

"I whole-heartedly welcome this book for its challenge
to practically apply our faith in the workplace, with the
strong conviction that as we work out our faith in the
hurly-burly of every-day life, we will find that God is
working alongside us."

Dr Bob Duerden, Senior Education Adviser, East Yorks

"*Exploring Your Vocation* is a superb resource for anyone
wanting to discover greater meaning in their working
life."

Rev Lyndon Bowring, Executive Chairman of CARE

"A vocation in work and life together is one of the most
important ways of giving us vision and direction in all we
do. Matt Bird has drawn this together in an imaginative
and readable way – a recommended read."

Sir John Stevens, Metropolitan Police Commissioner

First published in 2002 by Spring Harvest Publishing Division and Authentic Lifestyle

08 07 06 05 04 03 02   7 6 5 4 3 2 1

Authentic Lifestyle is an imprint of Authentic Media
P.O. Box 300, Carlisle, Cumbria, CA3 0QS, UK
and Box 1047, Waynesboro, GA 30830-2047
www.paternoster-publishing.com

British Library Cataloguing in Publication Data

A catalogue record for this book is available from the British Library

ISBN 1-85078-476-0

Cover design by Diane Bainbridge
Printed in Great Britain by
Cox and Wyman, Cardiff Road, Reading

Exploring Your Vocation

Stop Working and Start Living

by **Matt Bird** & friends

Foreword by Sir Brian Mawhinney MP

Thanks

To Johnny Sutherland, Shane Mullins, Stuart Oldroyd, Kay Barling, Sara Phillips, Andy Reed, Danny Shaw, Esther Bird, John Rollo and Dave Campbell. Thank you for your friendship and for sharing your inspirational lives and stories.

To Adam Eakins and the JoshGen team for developing the small group material.

To Steve Clifford, Jill Garrett, Don Latham, John Smith and Simon Warner for reading and commenting on the text.

Contents

Foreword

As I read and reread this book, three powerful messages emerged.

First, work is or should be service. I have spent many years claiming that my primary calling is to serve those who elected me, and the wider community, not just because I am a member of Parliament but also because I am a Christian. Matt Bird and his friends explore with conviction that commitment to service, to vocation more impressively than ever I could.

Secondly, this book is hugely encouraging. It highlights the fact that God does use ordinary people to affect positively the lives of others, to his glory. And it demonstrates that, despite what we may sometimes think, all of us have experiences and problems that are common to all Christians.

Finally, there is nothing theoretical in these pages. From the experiences recounted flow practical suggestions about how the shining realities in the lives of some can be our experience too. The ready-to-use small group sessions rob any church or group of the excuse that this issue is too difficult or complex to handle.

In his testimony, Dr John Rollo highlights our common experience and, sometimes, difficulty. 'The greatest challenge, however, does not lie in dealing with the public; they only meet Dr Rollo. Friends and colleagues meet John.' This book demonstrates that Jesus operates effectively in the professional and the person.

"Work as vocation?"

What a wonderful idea.

Rt Hon Sir Brian Mawhinney PhD MP

Introduction

Very few people don't have to work. Most do. Some
are obscenely well paid. Others don't get paid at all. In
between are those who receive a fair wage, those who
are poorly paid, and those who volunteer. Workers
can be employed or self-employed, full-time or part-
time. We do our work in places as varied as office, shop,
factory and school, from the home and in the home.

God gave work to us as one of the basic dimensions of
human life. One of the words the Bible uses for work
it also uses for worship, because worship is very closely
associated with service. Therefore worship is not only
about singing hymns and songs, but also about working
well. To put it another way – our lives are offerings of
living sacrifice to God (Rom. 12:2). Whatever we do,
we should work at it with all our heart as if working for
the Lord and not for men (Col. 3:23).

If God's design is for work to be worship, why is
work so far from that for so many people? I believe
it's because we get stuck with jobs that we do only to
earn money, because we need money to live. There's
nothing wrong with wanting to earn money to live – it
is essential. However, wouldn't it be good if we could do
that and more by getting a vocation rather than a job? It
is my personal conviction that there are three distinctive
aspects to being in a vocation rather than doing a job.

Firstly, vocation has a sense of "this is meant to be"
about it; a sense of rightness that might be described as
having an element of calling. The Bible talks about us
being created in Christ Jesus to do good works, which

God prepared in advance for us to do (Eph. 2:10). The vocational stories throughout *Exploring Your Vocation* all have that sense of divine destiny about them.

Secondly, vocation has a sense of contributing to society. In one of his most profound moments, the seventeenth century philosopher Rene Descartes declared *cogito ergo sum*, meaning 'I think, therefore I am'. Nowadays the spirit of our age is more likely to be defined as *tesco ergo sum*. meaning 'I shop, therefore I am'. Even though we need commodities such as food and drink to live, and other products develop our quality of life, consumerism is our *Zeitgeist*. However, Jesus said: 'If anyone would come after me, he must deny himself, take up his cross and follow me. For whoever wants to save his life will lose it, but whoever loses his life for me will save it' (Lk. 9:23-24). What Jesus said can be interpreted as the dictum 'I give, therefore I am'. So will we get a job that feeds our consumerism, or a vocation that contributes something to society?

These days, even public companies – driven by profit – ask questions about corporate and social responsibility rather than simply what is best for their shareholders. Staying with shops for a moment, Tesco's giving into communities through vouchers for school computers has resulted in increased profits, but that's another story.

Thirdly, vocation has a sense of a fit between my strengths and the demands of the work. The Gallup Organisation describes strength as 'consistent near-perfect performance in an activity'. This strength is made up of the knowledge and skills that have been acquired through life, and innate talent and identity.

Talent is defined as 'any recurring pattern of thought, feeling or behaviour that can be productively applied'. Research by Gallup shows that talent can be identified through the answers to several questions. What are your spontaneous reactions? What are your yearnings? What areas do you experience rapid learning in? What do you feel satisfaction in doing?

Peak performance in work is achieved through matching a person and their talents to a suitable job and responsibilities. There is no such thing as a person who isn't any good, only a mismatch between a person and their work.

It may be that your work doesn't fit who you are. In which case, I encourage you to explore new ways of working. This could mean a complete change of career, or a few changes to your job description at your next performance appraisal. Achieving your God-given potential or self-actualisation is important for knowing a sense of fulfilment and satisfaction in life.

As work consumes over 50 per cent of our waking lives, it is too important to be merely a job. It needs to be a vocation. I pray that as you read this book God will lead you into work that feels like it was meant to be, contributes to society, and fits your unique strengths and talents. I believe with all my heart that we can find God in whatever work we do – whether in family, community, education, health, politics, law, order, media, business or retail.

What follows are five steps to exploring your vocation, drawing from the biblical character of Joseph recorded in the book of Genesis, stories of people who have discovered something of what their vocation is, and ready-to-use sessions for small groups. I hope they encourage you in your vocation as much as they have encouraged me.

Please take the time to reflect on these words by Cardinal Newman, and then reread them to yourself as a prayer of declaration.

> *God has created me to do him some definite service; he has committed some work to me which he has not committed to another. I have my mission; I never may know it in this life, but I shall be told it in the next. I have a part in a great work; I am a link in a chain, a bond of connexion between persons. He has not created me for naught. I shall do good, I shall do his work; I shall be an angel of peace, a preacher of truth in my own place, while not intending it, if I do but keep his commandments and serve him in my calling.*

—1—

Exploring The Journey

The first step in exploring your vocation is to recognise that vocation is a journey. Vocation is not a destination you somehow arrive at; rather, it is a lifelong journey you embark on. Sometimes we can give the impression that we have 'arrived', but in reality God has only just begun.

Like all journeys, the direction of vocation is determined by the choices we make today. The options we will have available to us tomorrow are partly decided

Some journey along a super-fast highway, others along a pot-holed track, and others through an urban maze.

by the decisions we made yesterday. There are also many twists and turns on the journey of vocation over which we have no control, apart from the way we choose to respond to them. A friend of mine says we have no control over at least 80 per cent of what life throws at us, but we do have total control over how we respond.

Joseph's life and vocation was a long journey of ups and downs, of great favour and grand betrayal. He began as a favoured son (Gen. 37:1–11) before becoming a betrayed brother (37:12–36), then a favoured slave (39:1–6) before becoming a betrayed servant (39:7–20), then a favoured prisoner (40:1–23) before becoming a betrayed prisoner (39:21–23), then finally a favoured prime minister (41:39–43). How about that for a roller-coaster of a ride!?

Sometimes I felt that I had a clear idea of where I was going and why, but at other times God totally surprised me.

For every common hero and heroine in the Bible, vocation is a journey of choices and surprises, and unsurprisingly it is the same for us. Some journey along a super-fast highway, others along a pot-holed track, and others through an urban maze. Whatever the route, your vocation is not something you will arrive at overnight but an adventure that you can explore for the rest of your life.

My own vocational story is one of officer in the

Ministry of Defence, minister in the church, founder and director of a national charity, and most recently a councillor in local government. The different stages of my journey have overlapped, with past decisions limiting or liberating the options before me in the next. Sometimes I felt that I had a clear idea of where I was going and why, but at other times God totally surprised me. Being open is what matters.

"It doesn't seem to involve many grand schemes or global strategies; it seems to be far more about the little details."

The stories of how God takes a person into, and on in, their vocational journey are inspiring. Here is one such story, told by Johnny Sutherland, a police inspector at Fulham Police Station.

I guess my journey really started when I was 16 or 17, and something just clicked inside me. I was standing on Hammersmith Broadway – waiting for the bus to school – when I saw a policeman walking along on the other side of the road. He wasn't doing anything in particular – but something just clicked inside me.

Five or six years later, I turned up at Hendon in North London to start my training as a Metropolitan Police Officer. Since that morning at the bus stop I'd never really wanted to do anything else. And now I've truly got the best job in the world.

"I guess that I've simply followed my heart – trusting that the doors he opens no one can shut, and those that he shuts, no one can open."

I hadn't been woken in the night by angels and I didn't find a divine hand writing instructions on any walls. I wasn't even given any specific advice that had pointed me towards the police service. It was just that something had clicked inside.

In my own faltering way, I've always tried to journey with God and his design for my life. Beyond that, I guess that I've simply followed my heart – trusting that the doors he opens

no one can shut, and those that he shuts,
no one can open. Following him, and then
following my heart.

God is at work in the Metropolitan Police,
and in me as well. Sometimes I have big
dreams; but mostly it's about trying to follow
Jesus' example day by day. As I've journeyed
on, the one thing that has really struck me is
Locard's Principle. Locard's Principle is used
in the detection of every major crime. It states
simply: 'Every contact leaves a trace.' What
this means is that when two objects come into
contact with one another, an exchange takes
place. When a burglar smashes a window
and cuts himself, traces
of his blood and fibres
from his jumper will
be left at the scene.
Similarly, fragments
of broken glass will
be found all over his
clothing because every
contact leaves a trace.

"Somewhere underneath that cover of my uniform, Jesus crept in: Every contact leaves a trace."

I remember going to a
reported crime on one of
the estates in Peckham:
A lady living there had
had one of her windows
smashed. So I just went to do my job. As I
thought about it afterwards, I was struck by
the number of people in our society who are
afraid. There are bars and locks on windows

and doors – and people are sometimes scared to come out of their homes and afraid to let anyone in. And yet – on that particular afternoon – that lady let me into her home. Because of the uniform I was wearing and the job I was there to do. I wasn't there for long and didn't have too much to say. But I could try to do my job well and to show compassion and kindness along the way. And somewhere underneath that cover of my uniform, Jesus crept in: Every contact leaves a trace.

> "As I work out my vocation in whatever job, it's all about learning to love God and love my neighbour."

It struck me a while back that this principle actually applies to all human relationships – whenever two people come into contact an exchange takes place. This applies as much with those we encounter only in passing, as with those we've known for a lifetime. After meeting, we take something of them away with us and leave something of ourselves behind because every contact leaves a trace. And, if this principle holds true, the question (in life and in work) becomes – what kind of trace am I going to leave behind?

It's a question that urges me towards the life of Jesus Christ. As I work out my vocation in whatever job, it's all about learning to love God and love my neighbour. About becoming light in the darkness – with victims of crime, with prisoners in cells, with those injured in accidents, with the lost and the lonely.

It doesn't seem to involve many grand schemes or global strategies; it seems to be far more about the little details. Of simply journeying with Jesus day by day.

Johnny's journey starts early in life, because early experiences shape us and mould us into what we are today, and his path has taken him into one profession so far. The journey for Johnny continues – in 2002 he received a Metropolitan Police Commendation for his leadership through a very difficult incident. Shane Mullins, the managing director of Fiscal Engineers, tells a very different story of his vocational journey.

My journey to becoming a financial consultant and businessman has been far from straightforward. Looking at my life, it might appear like a random selection of jobs, but I believe that God has been in and through it all. I began my working life as a professional golfer - having taken up the game as a young lad. At the time, I was told I would never make it as a pro – but that just made me want to try even harder. I played as often as I could – and proved everyone wrong.

> *"I have come across some people who believe the financial sector is no place for Christians to be. I disagree."*

The decision to take up a new career was partly based on finance. Unless you make it as a top professional golfer, the game doesn't pay a lot. However, my time in golf meant mixing with successful businessmen and others who were financially secure. It initiated my interest in taking up a career as a financial advisor. The normal route into the profession is through a university degree. Then, conventional wisdom would suggest, you take up a graduate post in one of the big firms. My route was rather unconventional.

After a short time in business and with limited financial experience, I found myself taking over a small financial advisory practice. It wasn't in the best of shape – but determination, and I believe some help from God, led to the business being turned around. Two or three years later the firm was merged with a middle-sized Midlands based firm and I became a director, which gave me a lot more experience. The latest step in my journey led me to begin a new business venture – Fiscal Engineers Limited. As a company we specialise in giving advice to companies and individuals with large amounts of capital to invest.

I have come across some people who believe the financial sector is no place for Christians to be. I disagree. There are more references in the Bible relating to wealth than pretty much anything else. God wants to prosper us and also to use the money he entrusts us with wisely. I believe that a bank statement says more about a person's character and faith than the songs they sing and the prayers they pray. Through my work as an independent financial advisor, I am able to provide the advice people need – both professional and godly. My clients would be

> *"My clients would be described as very successful and yet they are people who often remain unfulfilled and have great needs."*

described as very successful and yet they are people who often remain unfulfilled and have great needs.

Shane's vocation isn't something he walked into when he left school, but it is something that he explored as a golfer, and independent financial adviser. Now he is exploring it as the managing director of an increasingly successful company.

You may like to continue exploring your vocation as a journey in a small group with the ready-to-use session opposite.

In a Small Group...

Materials required – film of *The Beach* or *Shrek*, Bibles, paper and pens.

Assemble

Journeys can be a good experience, like an exciting visit to see an old friend; or a bad experience, such as sitting in traffic or a delayed train. Think about journeys to work or during work that you have had, both good and bad, and tell the story to the group.

Use one of these films to introduce the topic of journeys.

The Beach – While backpacking in Thailand, Richard gets a map to a remote island where a small community lives. He tells his two French friends and they head off on a journey to discover this wonderful destination.

DVD — Chapters 8 and 9

VHS — 26min 33sec to 33min 20sec

Or

Shrek – Shrek is an agreeable enough ogre whose peace is disturbed by Lord Farquaad, who is evicting the local fairytale creatures to his swamp. To get the creatures moved he agrees to take a journey to rescue a princess for the lord to marry. This is where we join the story.

DVD — Chapter 5

VHS — 22min 50sec to 30min 10sec

Adore
The Bible is full of journeys – they are a key part of God's plan for all of us. Pause as a group at this point and use Psalm 23 to reflect on the Lord as a shepherd who leads us. You may want to write down prayers of praise to God, who leads us all in our vocational journeys.

Apply
Look at Genesis 37:12–36 and then consider the following issues. Encourage discussion to develop further understanding. You may want to refer back to the stories of Johnny Sutherland and Shane Mullins as part of the study.

❖ What are the key teaching points in the passage relating to the idea that we are on a vocational journey?

❖ What tough times in your working life can you now look back on and see how God was working?

❖ What work situations that you face cause you

to question, as Joseph may have, where God is and how this can work for good? Share your thoughts, and also consider what strength or encouragement can be gained from these verses.

Look at Genesis 39:2–6, 20–23 and 41:37–40. These verses continue the story.

❖ What are the key teachings that relate to being faithful in our vocational journey?

Action

Take an A4 sheet of paper and draw a horizontal line from one side to the other. This line represents your life so far. Think of the significant events in your life, such as education and relationships. On the line, write down your hopes and dreams relating to vocation. Now share these in pairs and give thanks for the journey so far. You could pray about your dreams for the future. Discuss with each other how you will begin to go after these dreams and make yourself accountable in these areas.

2

Exploring God's Worldview

Step two of exploring your vocation is to adopt God's view of the world – and in particular work. This can be described as his worldview. Another way of describing worldview is using the metaphor of a pair of glasses. Imagine that every person wears a pair of sunglasses and that each pair has a unique tint, so everyone sees some colours more strongly than others and some colours not at all. Worldview is the tint, or attitude, through which we view the world around us.

> *An excellent road sweeper is as pleasing to God as an excellent teacher.*

God's worldview is joined up, it is holistic and integrated, and it is one in which all people and all work (except what is illegal or immoral) are equally valued and important.

There is no hierarchy of value in God's eyes when it comes to work: an excellent road sweeper is as pleasing to him as an excellent teacher. There is no division into 'secular' work such as being a policeman or a managing director, and 'sacred' work such as being a vicar or a missionary. A dualistic worldview is not biblical and gives the impression that some work is of more interest to God and some is beyond his domain and influence. So if there is even a trace of dualistic sacred/secular worldview in us we had better find a way to get rid of it quick!

> "My job might not have the same obvious opportunity for changing people's lives as a teacher, social worker or charity worker but God can and does work through those of us in more commercial professions."

As the prime minister of Egypt (41:39–43), Joseph had a holistic life perspective. Joseph was the person through whom God would save the Hebrews from famine (42–45 esp. 45:4–7). The people of God in Old Testament times had no concept of life after death, and therefore to be saved was not a future hope but a present reality. There was no divide between the material world and spiritual world; the two were intertwined. With this holistic worldview the salvation of the people of God was as much an issue for politicians as for priests.

The world is a single integrated reality in which God sees all vocations as of equal value, whether they are property developer or mum. If this were not the case the only job worth doing would be that of evangelist, with the objective of getting people into heaven when they die. Rather, all work has an intrinsic value and is made sacred because of our attitude towards it.

Most people work to live, while workaholics live to work – and those with a godly worldview aspire to live and work as the rhythm of life.

Stuart Oldroyd, a land director with Taylor Woodrow, describes how he views his work.

My wife is a social worker and people are quick to see her role as a God-given vocation, however I sometimes need to explain mine. I have always been interested in buildings and property. The best buildings are truly inspiring – who hasn't stood in a cathedral, looked up at the roof and been amazed at the scale, the detail and the work that has gone into creating such an impressive place?

Few modern buildings are quite so inspiring, but the thrill of seeing a large-scale creation come about from your ideas and hard work is something I shall never grow tired of.

"I know that I am in the right industry, the right organisation and the right place."

I thought at first that I wanted to become an architect, but later became attracted to the breadth of the whole development process. It involves identifying a site, obtaining planning consent, getting it built and finally seeing occupiers add life to your creation by living and working in the spaces that you envisaged and helped bring about.

The best developments are enduring monuments to your own work that can be visited decades later, often mellowing into their surroundings and improving with age.

I worship a creator God, and I believe that making beautiful buildings has a worth in its own right. But for me, it isn't just about buildings, it's much more about people.

Each development is unique and involves a fresh challenge to be met by all sorts of different people. Each project involves different landowners, planners, engineers, contractors, builders, surveyors and many others. The common denominator is that as the project director, they all look to me for guidance.

Every project team is unique, each requiring different solutions, and I am responsible for a number of them, all at different stages in the development process. The need for effective leadership, understanding and decisiveness to meet every new challenge is stretching, demanding and ultimately incredibly fulfilling.

"I've often been surprised by the number of people who value and recognise true integrity."

Despite being a highly commercial activity, the focus on people and the daily interaction with a very broad variety of team members gives an opportunity to spread widely a taste of what it means to live for God. In a hothouse of demanding targets, high pressure, long hours, high rewards and an overriding commercial and financial focus, it is surprising how often people notice someone who has a different perspective.

Sometimes it is in simple things like language and attitude. Sometimes it is in showing an interest in people beyond just what they can offer to the project. Sometimes it is in a more obvious ethical or moral perspective that leads you to take a decision that isn't the easiest 'shortcut' and may not have the same personal advantages. Whatever the reason, people notice the refreshing and positive difference that comes from letting your relationship with God affect the way that you are at work and the way a project is undertaken.

"Nothing gives me greater pleasure than to tell people why I won't compromise."

Throughout the nine years I've been involved in property, I've often been surprised by the number of people who value and recognise true integrity. People often tell me that they see an honesty and trustworthiness that leads them to do business with me and my department, rather than with others; even when to do business with others might appear more lucrative. In the world of commerce these qualities are all too scarce. People are constantly prepared to sacrifice their integrity just to 'do the deal'. Nothing gives me greater pleasure than to tell people why I won't compromise. This has led to opportunities to share my faith in a context where actions have already spoken much louder than words ever could.

I know that I am in the right industry, the right organisation and the right place. My job might not have the same obvious opportunity for changing people's lives as a teacher, social worker or charity worker but God can and does work through those of us in more commercial professions. We can reach and influence people who might not otherwise come into contact with the rich and positive life that comes from living in a relationship with God.

> *Voluntary, unpaid work is of course of equally great value as any other work.*

Stuart's story speaks of the intrinsic value of work. The creative design of buildings (not just cathedrals) is pleasing to God, and so are ethical decisions even if they affect the bottom line and reduce profit. Most people work to live, while workaholics live to work – and those with a godly worldview aspire to live and work as the rhythm of life. Some work is voluntary, unpaid and from the home; and is of course of equally great value as any other work. Kay Barling tells her story as a mum.

As with all things there is a complex mixture of reasons and influences that shape our decisions, and becoming a full time mum at home was no different. Certainly I had a somewhat romantic view of floating around in my beautifully organised and efficient home, always remaining calm and unflustered by the demands of the day, being a fun mum who managed to encourage learning, create a home and be a devoted wife.

Well, that soon evaporated! The truth is that after 17 years of being in this vocation my reasons for staying at home remain the same: I want to give myself to raising our children. It was by no means a casual decision because it required my husband, Chris, and I to shape our lifestyle around it. The influences behind the decision were our strong belief in family life and our own experiences of growing up. We were very careful to make the decision together; we valued my being at home. A crucial factor was not only that Chris had to bring in an adequate income, but we were to regard this as ours rather than as his. I have never felt economically disempowered. I think often, staying at home

"God has been a tremendous source of help and comfort, solace and delight as I have been at home, often on my own."

can be seen as a cop out and less valuable than earning; but what greater privilege and responsibility is there than bringing up children yourself?

My faith in God has made a difference to my role on three levels. First, the Bible is full of a wonderful attitude to life that actually works particularly well in family: kindness, honesty and forgiveness. Jesus paid a great amount of attention to how we should treat and view each other. As a family we have tried with a varying amount of success to hold on to these principles. Second, I have found the help and support of my friends invaluable and their commitment to me has made such a difference. Third, my intimate relationship with God has been a tremendous source of help and comfort, solace and delight as I have been at home, often on my own.

> *"What better way to ask God to help us to devour our obstacle than to devour the chocolate cake!"*

When it comes to our faith we try to live honest and open lives with our children. They really help when it comes to making a sober assessment of oneself, and they are not at all taken in by religious language or good looking actions which are actually hypocritical. They are great. So prayer in our household is a risky business: we rejoice in answered prayer but do not explain away prayers that aren't answered as we would like. We have had a number of clear and stunning answers to prayer as well as some mysterious and difficult puzzles.

On one occasion our new software business was in desperate need of investment. We had included the children in our decision to start the business, as it would definitely affect their lives, and now it was in the balance. I wanted us to come before God as a family, but praying words when you are young is not always the easiest way. Over the years I have developed my own creative style of praying with our children, a more 'doing' kind of prayer. With that approach in mind I explained to the children that our business had an obstacle to get over, the obstacle of finding an investor. Earlier I had baked a chocolate cake and had placed chocolate money on the top and named it our prayer cake. The idea behind this being that our God helps us to devour obstacles, he calls us to be overcomers, and what better way to ask God to help us to devour our obstacle than to devour the chocolate cake! It was definitely the most enthusiastically embraced prayer meeting that I have ever attended.

> *"Am I just a 'mum at home'? No way!"*

What's more, just a couple of hours later we received a call from a company that connects entrepreneurs and investors. They gave us an opportunity to present our business and it was from that meeting weeks later that we met our first investor. What a wonderful faith-building experience for our children.

Being a mum at home has also given me a great opportunity to get involved with our children's schools, ranging from helping in the classrooms, being part of a prayer support group and becoming a parent governor. I have had the privilege of being able to get to know so many parents and children in my neighbourhood and that is something that I value highly. So am I just a 'mum at home'? No way! I am the careful owner of a challenging, provoking, hair tearing, frustrating, immensely fulfilling vocation.

You may like to continue exploring your vocation by examining God's worldview in a small group, using the ready-to-use session on the next page.

In a Small Group...

Materials required – film of *Being John Malkovich* or *The Truman Show*, Bibles, holiday snaps, glasses and download from the website www.joshgen.org

Assemble
On the website www.joshgen.org you will find many optical illusions to download and use. Either display them on a laptop if you have access to one, or print them out and hand them around. It's a fun way of discovering a new perspective and a good introduction into seeing a different worldview.

Use one of these films to introduce the topic of different worldviews.

Being John Malkovich – John Cusack's character starts a job as a file clerk. One day he accidentally discovers a portal into the brain of John Malkovich. This allows him to discover a different worldview.

DVD — Chapter 10

VHS — 25min 34sec to 32min 53sec

Or

The Truman Show – Jim Carrey plays Truman, who since birth has been the star of a TV show – but doesn't know it. His life is televised non-stop, but he does not realise that the town he lives in is a giant studio and that the world is watching his every move. We join the story as Truman begins to realise that all he has known about his life may not be true.

DVD — Chapter 8

VHS — 28min 16sec to 35min 26sec

Adore
Get some pictures of creation (for example, holiday snaps). There are some on the website www.joshgen.org that you can download. How do these pictures make you want to respond to God? How do they reflect God's personality? Read Colossians 1:15–20 and note how many times you see the words 'all things'. How does this help you to understand God's view of work? Praise God for being the God of all things, the invisible and the visible, the bits of creation we think are good as well as those we can hardly believe he could redeem.

Apply
Look at Genesis 45:4–7. Then consider the following issues and encourage discussion to develop further understanding. You may want to use Stuart Oldroyd's or Kay Barling's story as part of the study.

❖ What conflicts do you think Joseph faced as prime minister of Egypt because of his belief in the true God?

❖ Have you ever encountered a situation in your workplace where your Christian beliefs conflicted with the requirements of your job?

❖ Do you feel you can change the culture of your workplace so it better reflects the kingdom of God? If not get other people in your group to suggest ideas.

❖ What have you learnt so far from the story of Joseph that may have informed and changed your worldview?

❖ Looking at the example of Joseph, do you think there are any vocations that God wouldn't want us to be involved in?

Action

Many of us need to change our glasses and move away from a divided worldview, which separates sacred and secular work. We need to change our spectacles from bi-focals to single lenses so we see the world as God does. Use someone's in the group (or you can use the end of tumblers) and pass them around to see the difference they make to your view. How do we need to change our view in relation to what we have learnt in this study? If God is a God of all things, how will this change your attitude to work? What positive things does your organisation do? What could you do to make a difference in your workplace? Go on to ask people to share how this new God worldview could change things. After you have shared, encourage each person to place their hands on their own eyes. This is a simple outward sign of a change that we are asking God to make. To see the world the way God sees it.

—3—

Exploring Your Self-Understanding

The third step in exploring your vocation is to be committed to growing in self-understanding and awareness. The more we understand our God-given identity the better positioned we are to choose work that is congruent with that identity.

There are numerous dimensions and facets to our identity, some of which are innate and others the result of our nurture. Some nurturing experiences are good and some are bad, but

Experiences of life matured Joseph so that he could use his strengths in his vocation.

all have the potential to mature us. The different aspects of our identity can be summarised using an identikit that includes talent, personality, worldview, personal story, spirituality and relationships. Together these dimensions make us who we are.

In his early years, Joseph's strengths of honesty, favour, and interpreting dreams also showed up as weaknesses of telling tales (37:1–2), showing off (37:3–4) and arrogance (37:5–11). The experiences of life matured Joseph so that he could use his strengths in his vocation (40:8–19, 41:9–36). God intended Joseph's betrayal experience, through which his brothers intended to harm him, and all the other twists and turns of his journey 'for good' (50:20). God took Joseph's unique strengths and story and used them for his purposes.

> *"Ever since I can remember, poverty and injustice have moved me to tears."*

Sara Phillips is a trainee solicitor at Omerods in Croydon. Her vocational journey has been about discovering what she was created for.

It's amazing how my personal story, personality, worldview and talents have worked together in my vocation. My story starts when I was around eight years old, at the time of Live Aid. I can remember watching images of the Ethiopian famine and feeling so sad that I was watching people die of hunger in front of me, and so angry and helpless that I was powerless to stop it. Ever since I can remember, poverty and injustice have moved me to tears, compassion is an integral part of my personality. This provoked me to think, 'What can I do about this?' As a child and teenager it was very difficult because the answer tended to be, 'Not very much.'

> *"God used my personal experience to help me on the road to my vocation."*

I became a Christian when I was 15 years old, and rather than dampening any enthusiasm for the plight of the poor and oppressed, I found that my desire to help was increased. I became aware that God too has a deep compassion for the orphans, widows and aliens, and that what I was feeling was a faint echo of his heart. I felt I was sharing in some small way in his worldview. This general desire to help became a desire to work in human rights in my late teens although I still was not exactly sure what this would involve in practical terms.

I studied Latin American Studies at Warwick University, which involved a year out in Mexico City. Again, God used my personal experience to help me on the road to my vocation. While I was there I worked as a volunteer for a Mexican human rights organisation – working on cases of torture, disappearances and illegal detentions. It quickly became clear that without practical legal skills the amount I was able to do to help people was fairly limited. It was all very well feeling passionately about things and wanting to help, but I simply didn't have the technical expertise to make a difference. However, I also saw that while well-meaning lawyers tried to do their best, without God they quickly became swamped by the endless work and burned themselves out. I thought and prayed about the situation a great deal, and on returning to the UK decided to train as a lawyer so that my passion for justice could be directed and used by God. I wanted to be able to work technically at a high level, but with God's direction and help, and without losing my compassion for people. I needed to add skills to passion.

"I simply can't believe that it's me doing these things – it seems like a dream."

I have to say that I really disliked law school

and struggled with the discipline of doing something I didn't like for a time in order to do what I really wanted in the future. I also have to say that it was worth it. Since I started law, incredible doors of opportunity have opened that I simply could not have opened by myself. I barely had to apply for anything; things were pretty much just offered to me. Last summer (2001) I was able to work as a translator and legal caseworker for a Christian human rights organisation in Honduras and Bolivia, working alongside street children and for the land rights of an indigenous people group. I was also able to attend a conference at the United Nations in New York.

"It was all very well feeling passionately, but I didn't have the technical expertise to make a difference."

This year I spent some time in Rwanda working for the office of the prosecutor general on genocide cases. In one hundred days in 1994 around a million people were killed by possibly up to another million people in Rwanda. This genocide was carefully planned and organised by the top levels of society. It has left the country utterly traumatised and struggling to continue with ordinary life. The task of bringing to justice those who participated in the genocide is a monumental one, particularly for a nation that was one of the world's poorest even beforehand. For Rwanda to recover, there must be a sense that justice has been done, which thus far has not been the case. For three months I worked alongside the lawyers from the Rwandan government and a legal advisor from the US on issues to do with the genocide – particularly on helping develop the new system of Community Courts designed to speed up the trials of the 115,000 or so people languishing in Rwandan prisons. It was an amazing opportunity, but also an incredibly harrowing experience.

> *"I want to be expert at what I do in a professional sense, but to never lose sight of why I started this vocation."*

It has been amazing – I simply can't believe that it's me doing these things – it seems like a dream – and I'm not even fully qualified as a lawyer yet! I still have another two years until I qualify, and it is hard because it means another two years doing something that I don't completely love. However, having had a foretaste of what it is like to be able to do what I was created for, I am willing to wait and learn. One of the real issues in the area of international justice is that most people start out wanting to change the world, and after a while become disillusioned and either turn away from it, or start to see it only as a job and career to advance in. I know that as Christians we are not immune from this, but I also believe that with all the resources that God has to offer it is possible to make a difference in this area. I want to be expert at what I do in a professional sense, but to never lose sight of why I started this vocation; simply because God loves the poor and the oppressed and he has called me to be a voice for those who have no voice.

Sara describes finding what she was created for; and her vocation combines many elements that make it just right for her. Sara recognises, however, that vocation is a journey which can be costly at times, and she needs to learn and equip herself for a couple of years in order to truly work out her vocation. Andy Reed, the MP for Loughbrough, has the same passion for injustice, but in his case it took him down a totally different and completely unexpected route.

> *Vocation is a journey which can be costly.*

As a lad living in the sticks who wasn't especially academic, becoming an MP was definitely the last thing on my mind. However, I did develop an interest in politics through my youth group. Whilst other youth groups tended to play table tennis and footie the one that I went to invited visitors to speak about particular issues. It was the time when there were pictures of the starving in Africa at the same time as stories about European food mountains, and the injustice of it all made me passionate.

> *"It was suggested that we should write to our member of Parliament, but I felt that wasn't enough."*

It was suggested that we should write to our member of Parliament but I felt that this wasn't enough, so at the tender age of 17 I joined the Labour Party. It was 1983, probably the worst time to join the party.

I turned up and looked keen and ended up as chairman of the Constituency Party within a couple of years, and later I did a degree in public administration with the aim of taking up a vocation as a local government officer. I had no ambitions beyond that, because I was under the impression that somehow MPs were in another league. However, in 1992 people suggested that I should stand for the

Loughborough seat where I was chair of the constituency. It was totally unwinnable but I thought that it would be good to be able to tell my grandchildren that I had stood for Parliament the year that Labour came back to power under Neil Kinnock (how wrong you can be!). Still, I was pleased to cut the Conservative majority from 17,000 to 10,000.

People suggested that I look for a safe seat, but I wasn't interested as I had got married and settled down and would only fight for the seat where I lived. But then there was a boundary change around the village where I lived, and I found myself living in a new constituency with a really marginal seat. So I was asked to stand again as I had done so well last time. There was definitely no blinding flash of light, but at each stage opportunities arose almost without me having to push for them, and in 1997 I was elected. So God combined my desire for justice, my interest in politics and my personal circumstances to make me an unlikely MP.

> *"Everything I do is based on compassion and on a moral and ethical foundation."*

As an MP I have found there are expectations from the constituency and from Christians that I will have certain views. I am continually working at breaking out from the labels that I am given. As Christians we need to engage in a wide range of issues. Unfortunately we have been seen as only being interested in abortion, euthanasia and sexuality, and so we get marginalised as a right-wing sect. I have also had letters from Christians who are simply anti-everything, which can be so negative and destructive. I actually think that debt is a big moral issue – 24,000 children a day are dying because of it. So I was really encouraged when churches took a lead in the Jubilee 2000 campaign and I have tried to make a positive contribution in a number of other areas such as asylum.

There is a lot of pressure to be seen to be different as Christians and I try to be different both in my standpoint on issues and personally in the way that I approach things. Everything I do is based on compassion and on a moral and ethical foundation, rather than just looking at the arguments – a combination of heart and brain. I'm not going to stand in the House and say 'As a Christian …' when discussing the Integrated Transport Policy, but there are some things where I do give a Christian perspective.

I think a specific time when I really saw God at work was approaching the general election in 2001. When you are an MP you have put your life into service and it really is a vocation, so when you are fighting an election you are fighting not just for your party but for your job. People kept on asking me why I seemed so calm and happy, and the answer to that had to be that my life ultimately is centred on God and that I trusted him to have plans for me whether or not that involved another term in Parliament.

One of the great things about being a Christian MP is that we unite around Christ even though our views on policy differ so much. On the night of the election I was waiting for the results to come through with all the local Labour Party supporters and heard that a Christian friend from another party had won her marginal seat. I got some very strange looks as I spontaneously cried, 'Yes!'

> *"I sometimes wonder why I am here, but when I look at the bigger picture I know."*

When I am traipsing back to my flat at 3am in the morning, having debated on some strange procedural motion, I sometimes wonder why I am here, but when I look at the bigger picture I know – it is vitally important to have Christians who are not afraid to speak up for the poor, vulnerable and oppressed in places of influence.

Andy has discovered who he is – someone with compassion for the marginalized, who likes to debate and believes in public service. His personality and talents mean that he can best serve God as a member of Parliament.

You may like to continue exploring your vocation by looking further at your self-understanding in a small group using the ready-to-use session opposite.

In a Small Group...

Materials required – film of *Bridget Jones's Diary* or *East is East*, Bibles and pen/paper.

Assemble

Ask everyone to write down one piece of information about themselves that no one else will know. Fold the piece of paper and place it in a pile with everyone else's. Then take it in turns to take a piece of paper and read out what has been written. The group is to try and decide who wrote the statement. When you have two left, read them out together to avoid making it obvious who is left.

Use one of these films to introduce the topic of knowing yourself.

Bridget Jones's Diary – Bridget has just found out that Daniel, her dream man but also her boss, has been two-timing her. We join her as she goes to see him the day after learning of his treachery. This leads her to sort out her life.

DVD — Chapter 15–17

VHS — 42min 26sec to 48min 41sec

Or

East is East – George Khan is a proud Pakistani and rules his family with a rod of iron. He wants his two oldest sons to have arranged marriages, but one of them has not agreed. Here we see them talking about this and about his son's identity as a mixed race Anglo-Pakistani man.

DVD — Chapter 13

VHS — 1hr 10min 20sec to 1hr 13min 33sec

Adore

Use these verses (Job 33:4 and Is. 64:8) to consider the fact that we are the greatest part of God's creation and we are amazing in so many ways. You may want to write out the verses and ask people to write their names in the blanks. For example: 'The Spirit of God has made [*insert person's name*]; the breath of the Almighty gives [*insert person's name*] life.'

You could also get into twos and pray these verses over each other. Find some amazing facts about us as human beings and share them with the group, then use Psalm 139:13–16 to give praise and thanksgiving to our Father for his amazing creation.

Apply

You may want to use the story from Sara Phillips or Andy Reed as part of the study.

Look at these verses and build up a personality profile of Joseph in the way the police would with a suspect, or as you would with something like the Myers-Briggs personality test. Examine both the good and bad aspects, and discuss how God used them in the story.

Gen. 37:1–2

Gen. 37:3–4

Gen. 37:5–11

Gen. 39:5–10

Gen. 40:8–15

Gen. 41:14–40

Gen. 45:1–7

❖ Understanding who you are is an important part of this vocational journey and even in your difficult times God is working for good. Look at Genesis 50:20. Discuss how God used Joseph's experiences.

❖ Share with one another the experiences in your life, both good and bad. How is God using them in your vocational journey? You may want to take time out at this point to pray for each other.

Action

Everyone write their name at the top of a piece of paper and then pass it around to each person in the group. Ask everybody to write one of that person's strengths on it. When you have all received back your original pieces of paper, share in pairs what people have written and then pray in thanks and ask God to use these strengths as you continue in your vocational journey.

—4—

Exploring God's Will

Step four in exploring your vocation is to know God's will, which is easier than it sounds.

A helpful metaphor for understanding the will of God is a child playing in a park. The child has freedom to play anywhere in the adventure park because there are fences at the edges to protect the child from danger. That is what the will of God is like in Christ – there is freedom to choose. The will

The will of God is not restrictive.

of God is not like a tightrope that we have to walk, and when we falter and fall it is to certain disaster.

Picturing the Garden of Eden is also helpful in understanding God's will. Humankind was put in the garden to work it and was given freedom to eat from any tree except one (2:15–17). This is how the will of God works; he doesn't say there is only one tree we must eat from, rather that there any many trees we may eat from. The will of God is not restrictive; it is liberating.

In the context of work, we are not God's puppets but God's partners and there are numerous occupations in which we can work well and make a contribution to society.

"I am representing the company, but I am also representing Jesus."

As we have already seen, Joseph's life was full of good times and bad times. One of the greatest credits to his character was that whatever the experience in life he remained faithful to partnering with God even as a betrayed son (37), servant (39) and prisoner (40).

God guides us by providing freedom and boundaries through the Bible, the advice of wise and godly friends, peace that comes through prayer, and circumstances and opportunities.

Danny Shaw, a retail assistant at an electrical store in Huddersfield, tells the story of knowing the freedom and guidance of God in his vocation.

So how did I get where I am? I could have had a divine encounter with God or blinding revelation whilst prayerfully reading the Bible, but I didn't. Quite simply, at a time when I was looking for a job, a friend mentioned that there was one going at the shop where he worked. So I applied, went for two interviews and was offered the job. I didn't feel that I had a life-long calling to work in retail, but now I am there I love it and find I can serve people in this situation.

To me, my faith is measured most not by what I do at a church meeting or with friends but by what I am at work. Every time I walk into work I am representing the company but I am also

God guides us by providing freedom and boundaries.

representing Jesus and the difference this makes is really motivational. The whole of life is built around different relationships and I certainly have a lot of those in retail! For me, being a Christian at work is all about my outlook on what matters and attitude to people: my attitude to customers, colleagues and managers.

When I have been standing up all day and my feet are killing me, my sales figures are down and I am talking to a really boring customer who I know full well isn't going to buy anything, then it can be hard to treat people well. However, in this situation I remember the company's charter to deliver the best and to make a difference. I listen to each individual and attempt to meet and match their needs rather than simply trying to sell them the most expensive item.

When I'm not busy and see a colleague weighed down with carrying goods to the cash desk or struggling to make a sale then I try to go the extra mile to help them. Sometimes this is practical by giving them a lift to their bus station after a late shift, sometimes it's just by smiling or listening to them off-load. You never know what sort of day people have had or what might be happening at home.

> *"I know that I'll never be Bill Gates or Billy Graham, and I don't want to be."*

When my manager tells me to get a duster to clean stock then how do I react? It's the job I hate most and it would be easy to do it half-heartedly or resentfully. However, I try and remember that whatever I do I work at it with all my heart as if working for God. It's also not about me, it's about others, team work and delivering the best service possible.

I've been talking about small differences that

my faith makes in the workplace, however lots of small differences can make one huge difference. I look to have the perspective that I am an ambassador of Christ and not one of wanting to promote self. The best thing that I have learnt in retail is to be me, because that's the way that God created me to be. I want to be a 24/7 Christian rather than a Sunday Christian who's all show and no character. When the pressure is on that's when my faith really helps and I get noticed for being different. I know that I'll never be Bill Gates or Billy Graham, and I don't want to be. For me it's not about miraculous healings, confrontational evangelism or ruling the world, I simply want to excel in serving others. That is my vocation.

We are not God's puppets but God's partners and there are numerous occupations in which we can work well.

Danny found himself in his vocation as a retail assistant simply by circumstances. There he partnered with God to serve his stakeholders – customers, colleagues and managers – in small ways. Esther Bird, an assistant head teacher, tells the story of how God challenged her in a dream.

My story begins with a dream I had. During the eight years I'd been teaching I'd often had work-related dreams; however this dream was different.

I was teaching a class of children who were extremely challenging. The class was out of control, aggressive and unruly. Throughout the dream I was trying to discipline and control them and I tried desperately to restore order, but every strategy failed. In fact, the children's behaviour became worse and worse! When I woke up I felt exhausted and relieved that it had all been a dream. I sensed God was reminding me that I needed him when I'm at work and that it is he and I together making a difference. I realised that I'd become used to my work and I'd forgotten that to do it well I needed God's help. I went off to work and thought nothing more about it.

God can even speak and guide us through normal things like dreams.

The next day I received a phone call from one of the county education advisers, asking me if I would be prepared to work for one week in another school. I had already heard about the school, because it had failed its OFSTED (Office for Standards in Education) inspection and was under Special Measures.

This means that every term the school is visited by government inspectors and has to be seen to be making progress. A school is given two years to get itself out of Special Measures. I agreed, and then I remembered my dream and felt this might be significant.

On the Monday morning the children arrived and as far as they were concerned I was 'just another supply teacher' and easy prey. Approximately half of the class wanted to do as they pleased and were obviously not going to listen to what I had to say. I had not encountered such children before, they were outwardly aggressive towards others and clearly had little or no respect for me as an adult or as a teacher.

> *God doesn't say there's only one tree we must eat from, rather that there any many trees we may eat from.*

The day was very testing, and ended with the worst lesson I've ever tried to teach. I attempted to take a PE lesson, but once the class was outside they were like animals! They were tearing around, fighting each other and kicking the balls over the fence. I could not get them to stand still and listen to me. At the end of the day I felt it was the worst school I had ever visited and there was no way I would ever consider working somewhere like that. I couldn't wait to get back to my own school.

However, by the third day I was beginning to make progress. By being calm and positive I was having an effect. I realised that many of the children had desperately low self-esteem and were used to people shouting at them, telling them how rude and how useless they were, at school and at home. God was helping me to keep positive and not take their behaviour personally and this was transforming them fast.

When the inspectors arrived they came straight to my classroom. (They had visited only six weeks previously and the children were at that time, in their words, 'on the verge of rioting'.) The class was responsive and controlled and allowed me to teach them. They took turns instead of shouting out and tried hard during the individual work. The inspectors were delighted to see how they had improved.

"I knew that the job was for me, I had no doubt about it, although I was still apprehensive."

Despite the progress I was making, I still disliked the atmosphere of the school and was tired of the constant battle for control. Again I told God that I could never work in a school like this. At the

same time the stand-in head teacher asked
me if I would consider working at the school
from the new school year if a vacancy became
available. I was unsure and said it would have
to be the right job. At the end of the week the
children were told that I couldn't stay because
I had my own class of children; and tough as
I thought they were, two of the boys cried! I
felt guilty leaving and concerned about the
children's future, but I
was relieved to go.

"It was definitely

Three months later a job
advertisement appeared
for an assistant head at
the failed school. It was

worth the risk."

asking for somebody who'd teach within the
school but also somebody who'd be able to
work alongside the other teachers, helping
them to develop and encouraging excellence
within the school. After some thought I
applied for the job.

When I arrived for the interview, I was the
only candidate! At this stage I knew that
the job was for me, I had no doubt about it,
although I was still apprehensive about the
risk involved in going to a failing school. I
accepted the job.

At the end of my first year and five inspection
visits the school was removed from Special
Measures. The children want to learn and they
have a new pride in their school. The teachers

have made huge progress and the results within the school are clear. The previous year the SAT results for Year 6 had been so poor the school was placed at the bottom of the government league table for the county. By the following year, however, the results had improved by an average of 20 per cent.

Working at this school during this troubled time was great, it was rewarding and exciting to be involved in helping to transform a school, and together with the rest of the staff and God's help we did it. It was definitely worth the risk.

God can even speak and guide us through normal things like dreams. Esther's story shows that he can also challenge us to work in places we wouldn't normally consider.

You may like to continue exploring your vocation by discussing how God guides in a small group using the ready-to-use session opposite.

In a Small Group...

Materials required – film of *O Brother, Where Art Thou?* or *The Family Man*, Bibles, objects to be drawn and pen/ paper.

Assemble

Ask people to pair off and then ask each pair to sit with their backs to each other. Let them decide who is going to describe an object, and who will draw it (you can download these from the website www.joshgen.org). In the allowed time the drawer must draw what is on your piece of paper based on your description. You can't describe what the object is, only different length lines and shapes. The drawer can't speak during the first round. After the time is up you can compare results and swap roles. This time the person doing the drawing can ask questions of the other person as they describe the shapes. Talk about how the will of the describer affects the drawer and what difference it makes when we are in dialogue. Are we just following direct instructions from God, or is it a two-way dialogue?

Use one of these films to introduce the topic of exploring God's will.

O Brother, Where Art Thou? – George Clooney stars in this offbeat drama about three convicts on the run, seeking the money that is going to set them up for life. They have escaped the chain gang and are evading pursuit as we join them.

DVD — Chapter 2

VHS — 4min 30sec to 8min 10sec

Or

The Family Man – Jack (Nicolas Cage) is offered a job in London that will be great for his career, but will mean leaving his girlfriend. We see him at the airport with his girlfriend, having to make the decision as to which way his life is will go.

DVD — Chapter 1

VHS — 40sec to 3min 9sec

Adore
Look at Jeremiah 29:11. Give thanks to God for the truth of this verse and the fact it gives us confidence in God's will for our lives. Use songs of worship to express this if you wish.

Apply
Look at Genesis 50. Consider the following issues and encourage discussion to develop further understanding. You may want to use the story from Danny Shaw or Esther Bird as part of the study.

❖ There is a story told where a boy is creating chaos by searching every single Mars bar in a newsagents. Challenged, he explains that his mum told him she thinks one has his name on it. It a silly story, but it brings out the point that we would never say God has just one Mars bar for us and we must search it out, or there is only one type of chocolate just for us. No, there are many places to buy a chocolate and many varieties to choose from. We have a say and we can make choices.

❖ Why can this be the same as vocational decisions?

❖ If this is true of vocation, then there are numerous occupations in which we can work well and make a difference for God. Our vocation is not a game of chess in which we are pawns on the board and God is the player moving us. Try to think of a better description of God's will.

❖ We see the end of a great story in this chapter. What are the key points as we reflect on the many characters in this story in relation to God's will? Discuss the decisions that they made and the outcomes. How does this relate to the will of God and our vocational journeys?

Action

Take a piece of paper and draw a large square. In that square write all your interests, hobbies, passions and vocational dreams and then share them with one another. Now offer them to God and ask him to partner you as you enter the field, ready to go and play.

—5—

Exploring The Opportunities

The fifth step in exploring your vocation is to know the massive needs and opportunities in society. It is not so much a question of 'where can I make a difference?' as one of 'where am I not going to make a difference?'. The society and world in which we live is so full of needs and opportunities that we have a lot of freedom to choose where to make a difference.

> *Joseph continually saw the needs and seized the opportunities.*

Christians often shy away from the world, because they see it as corrupt and evil. The world is the object of God's love, however, and he wants to transform not condemn (Jn. 3:16–17). What better way to do that than through our working lives?

Joseph lived a life in which he continually saw the needs and seized the opportunities. Joseph was promoted through Potiphar's household as a slave (39:3–6) and then in prison he was put in charge of the other prisoners (39:21–23). In politics he became the prime minister (41:39–48). He didn't wait until he was in a strong position before showing initiative and taking responsibility; rather he saw the needs and opportunities where he was and acted.

There are so many places where Christians can make a positive, lasting and significant contribution to society through their vocation: whether it is education, which is facing the greatest teacher shortage for over 30 years; or local and national politics, which desperately need more men and women not only of ability but of integrity and character; or the media, which need more people who recognise their responsibility to avoid sensationalism; or business, which needs entrepreneurs to create enterprises that contribute to society; or homes and families, which need to know greater stability and love. Just do it!

John Rollo is a doctor in the army. He faced a number of choices between different vocational opportunities.

For me, the journey into medicine started quite late on. There was no desire as an infant to find the cure for cancer, nor a need to help the unreached masses of the African Plain. I got good grades and had a simple choice between law or medicine, and I chose the latter.

Despite this, God had his hand in those events and, more importantly, where I studied. A summer of camps, prayer and the advice of friends led me to believe that St Andrews University was the only teaching establishment in the Free World. I felt increasingly like God was steering me there – sometimes it felt more like shoving. When the offers were returned and St Andrews gave me an unconditional acceptance it was clear I'd end up there. The medicine part of things seemed sorted but there was a real problem, I wanted to be a soldier.

> *"If God had used a sledgehammer to open the doors of my mind his point would have been gentler made."*

On a cold August night (I was living in Scotland) there came a knock on our door. Standing there was a very dear family friend whom we hadn't seen for years. He had since joined the army as a chaplain. He explained that he'd felt he should visit us that night but had been too busy, until a series of road traffic accidents (all involving him) had forced him to seek refuge. Visiting from Edinburgh, ours was the nearest house. To my delight and my mother's horror he began to recount the need for Christians in the armed forces. Here were 300,000 men and women working in the toughest environments on earth. Their welfare and care was the responsibility of only a handful of officers, the main ones being the medical officer (doctor) and the chaplain. If God had used a sledgehammer to open the doors of my mind his point would have been gentler made. I'd realised that it was possible to choose to be in a profession I enjoyed in an environment that I longed for. I knew that I wanted to be a doctor in the army. Tough days lay ahead.

> *"Medicine is a profession of knives – those in your hand and those in your back."*

It would be easy to say that I make a difference for God every day in the treatment of the sick and injured. I currently work for the British Army in a busy A&E department just off the M3. I do actually save lives, maybe even every day. Every person you come into contact with, you effect in some way. I hope for the majority of those people I display

Jesus Christ's love, but it is difficult treating every person as he did.

The greatest challenge however, does not lie in dealing with the public; they only meet Dr Rollo. Friends and colleagues meet John. Graduating as a doctor, you are taught to believe you are the bee's knees. You get a shiny white coat, a stethoscope and the title of doctor. You also become fair game to the staff of the hospital.

Joseph didn't wait until he was in a strong position before showing initiative and taking responsibility.

The challenge is to make a difference to these lives, and that has to come from example. There has to be a balance and I'll freely admit that more often than not I get it wrong. A junior doctor drives the social life of the hospital, and all too often gets caught up in it. I trust and pray though that honesty and integrity, along with a genuine love for my friends, will always be displayed.

My job is very stressful. I deal with all members of the community at all stages of their lives. I have to present diagnoses and prognoses to the young and old, and at all times I have to please my bosses. Medicine is a profession of knives – those in your hand

and those in your back. Everyone competes to do and look better than his or her colleagues. On top of this you feel you are constantly put down by the government and sought out by the staff of the hospital.

I remember clearly one elderly lady who on her admission to hospital told me of her faith in God. I had to sit by her bed one week later and tell her that her body was riddled with cancer and she would soon die from its effects. She merely smiled and asked me to pray with her. I spent a good hour with her, having one of those open, slightly watery-eyed prayer sessions where you both enjoy a conversation with God. As I left she smiled and asked if I had any messages for my grandparents. I said only that I loved them and would see them some day soon. An hour later I was asked to certify her death. My faith helped not only me but also that lovely lady in her last afternoon. Sometimes this job allows the greatest moments of sharing and friendship.

John faced numerous opportunities in his vocation and settled for only two. His story tells of the opportunity and challenge of being an example in our working lives. Dave Campbell, an accredited legal executive at Mark Williams Associates in Guildford, tells a wonderful story of the opportunities he faces each day.

As a young teenager I spent my time hanging around with friends in my home town, getting into various scrapes, and inevitably this led to contact with the local police. I remember the contempt that some of these officers showed to us – an attitude which only encouraged a similar attitude towards the police within my peer group.

At the age of 17 I had a life-changing experience with Jesus Christ. A couple of years later I left college, and a few months after that, after a series of wrong choices, I found myself out of work and unsure what I should be doing with my life. I remember getting down on my knees and praying to God for help. As I was praying the phone rang and a friend told me that he had been praying for me and thought that I should apply to work for his brother – who was a solicitor.

I successfully applied for the position and started work as an office junior. Five years later I was managing a very busy criminal law caseload, working day and night representing those arrested and accused of criminal offences. These people are often feeling vulnerable, valueless and ostracised by both their family and society.

I believe God loves them as people and that they deserve to be shown dignity and respect. I find my work a wonderful opportunity to be a friend to the friendless whilst they face either the consequences of their actions – or the trauma of being falsely accused of a crime.

I often walk into police stations to represent young people that form part of a broken generation in today's society. When family breakdown deprives young people of father figures, it is all the more important that the teachers, police officers, social workers and other authority figures that they have contact with show them the respect and dignity and compassion that every person deserves.

I now work for a criminal law firm based in Surrey. Whilst endeavouring to be excellent in our work as lawyers, we are also looking for opportunities to help our clients leave the circle of misery, crime and drugs that they are caught up in. God wants to give them a new start through Jesus Christ and we encourage those with addiction problems to get help from specialist rehabilitation centres.

I recall representing a young man at Snaresbrook Crown Court in London. He was charged with the importation of cannabis from Holland. I had been told that he was a tough guy and not someone to turn your back on. But when I visited him for the first time in Chelmsford Prison I saw that something had changed in him. As we discussed his case in the cells below the court I felt prompted to tell him that God had a wonderful plan for

his life and his eyes began to fill with tears.
He told me that before his arrest, as he had
been travelling on the ferry from Holland,
he had started to pray to God, telling him
that something pretty drastic would have to
happen to him if he were to start to follow
him. A few hours later he had been arrested
and remanded in custody. Today he, his wife
and their church community run a drug
rehabilitation centre in Hampshire.

It seems to me that in life there are no distinct
groups of 'righteous' and 'guilty' people but
instead only two sorts of guilty people, those
who know their guilt and those who deny
it. Often the inmates of prisons and the
criminals in society are closer to the former.

We have seen a number of people's lives
transformed. I know that God has called me
to this vocation and my hope is that many
others will sense that calling to show God's
love in police stations, courts and prisons of
the land.

There are so many vocational opportunities and needs,
yet we have only one life to live so we had better get on
with meeting the needs and seizing the opportunities.
What needs and opportunities are you responding to?

You may like to continue exploring your vocation by
looking at the opportunities available to you in a small
group using the ready-to-use session overleaf.

In a Small Group...

There is a whole wide world out there and so many needs and opportunities. How do we decide what ones we should respond to? We need to know how to *know* the needs and opportunities and consider a godly response. We will examine how Joseph responded and what we can learn from that. Materials required – film of *The Shawshank Redemption* or *Billy Elliott*, Bibles and pen/paper.

Assemble

Prepare for this part of the meeting by buying some national and local newspapers and giving them out to the group. Ask the group to look through the papers and identity needs and opportunities from some of the stories and the job vacancies. Share them with the whole group and then discuss them.

Use one of these films to introduce the topic of seeing the needs and opportunities.

The Shawshank Redemption – City banker Andy Dufresne (Tim Robbins) arrives at Shawshank State Prison to serve a life sentence for a murder he didn't commit. He links up with the prison 'fixer', Red (Morgan Freeman). We will see them talking about their hopes and dreams. Andy finds that survival comes down to a simple choice, get busy living or get busy dying.

DVD — Chapter 15

VHS — 1hr 36min 20sec to 1hr 42min 45sec

Or

Billy Elliott – This is an amazing story of the eleven-year-old son of a coal miner in northern England during the 1984 miners' strike. Billy (Jamie Bell) has a chance meeting with the ballet class and he shows a natural talent. His teacher wants him to give the Royal Ballet a go, but that is not easy when his Dad and brother still think he is taking boxing lessons.

DVD — Chapter 4

VHS — 13min 49sec to 19min

Adore
Continue to look at the newspaper articles and pray into the areas, asking that God would send people who know him to these needs and opportunities to make a difference. Give thanks and praise for these opportunities. Use John 3:16 and 2 Corinthians 5:16–21 to focus your heart on God attitude towards the world.

Apply
Look at Genesis 39:3–6, 39:20–23 and 41:41–45. Then consider the following issues and encourage discussion to develop further understanding. You may want to use the story from John Rollo or Dave Campbell as part of the study.

❖ What are the key teaching points to learn from this story that relate to discovering the needs and opportunities concerning the workplace God may be drawing you to?

❖ What things hold you back from responding to these needs and opportunities?

❖ How can we find out more about the needs and opportunities in the workplace God may have for us?

Action
In pairs share one need or opportunity you have discovered recently, and pray about how you can begin to impact it. If you are unable to think of any, pray that God will reveal them to you. You may want to make yourself accountable to others in the group in regards to making a difference after all you have been challenged with during these studies.

Conclusion

The church, like the human body, is amazing in all
its variety. Each person is totally unique in his or her
talents and personality, upbringing and circumstances.
Ever seen a human body made up of ears? This picture
of the church also demonstrates that we all need each
other to function at our best and support one another
in whatever work we're doing. We need to lose the
hierarchy of some forms of
work being viewed as more
holy than others – where
at the top of the scale are
congregational leaders
and missionaries, and at
the bottom lie business
people, politicians and traffic
wardens.

> *Every person*
>
> *journeying with*
>
> *Jesus is in full-time*
>
> *Christian work*
>
> *—whatever job they do.*

It's true that some
people are called to be
congregational leaders, and
their role is to envision, equip and empower the church
to live for Jesus in their households, neighbourhoods
and workplaces (Eph. 4:11–12). But others are called to
be doctors, retail assistants, parents, actors, politicians,
charity workers, and the list goes on. Every person has

a God-given destiny for his or her life, to do what they are good at and to use their talents in work that fits who they are.

Every person journeying with Jesus is in full-time Christian work whatever job they do, and every Christian is a missionary in their workplace. There's no such thing as a part-time Christian. You are just as much a Christian – living out what it means to be church – at home or work as in a congregational meeting. Forget about telling the church to get out into the world – we already live there and work there.

Jesus once said that the harvest was plentiful, but the workers few (Lk. 10:2). Until now the workers have remained few because congregational leaders were the only ones viewed as being God's workers. The day is long overdue when every person sees their work as sacred, whatever sector of society it is in, however large or small the role. So have fun exploring your vocation.

Appendix A

Congregational Ideas

Perhaps one of the questions you are asking, or
are beginning to ask, is how can this integrated
understanding of work and faith affect my church
community? Below is a list of tried and tested ways
that church communities have used to begin to
respond to that same question. If you have tried other
ideas that have worked please do let me know at
mattbird@joshgen.org

Tell Stories

Ask a couple of people to talk about their
work and what difference being a Christian
makes. Less confident people can be
interviewed. This may mean reducing the
length of the sermon/talk, the sung worship
and/or other elements.

Biblical Teaching

Form a group to plan the biblical teaching for meetings, and make the majority people from the workplace. It might also be good to use this group to discuss how the Bible is used.

Using the Bible

Form a group to discuss these questions: How well does it work to ask a 'professional' Bible handler to explain what the Bible says and then try and apply it to real life? How would it be for people to provide the context of workplace or household and use the Bible to interpret experiences in those places?

Review Meetings

Review the purpose or meetings and ask whether people are serving meetings or meetings are serving people. Review the length and frequency of meetings and ask whether you could meet fortnightly and share stories of how you used the freed up time the previous week.

Attend a Conference

For example, register for a Spring Harvest *At Work Together* conference for equipping Christians for the workplace so you can develop your understanding of faith and work and meet others in similar workplaces.

Skills

Find out what talents people are already using in the workplace, then use them appropriately in the congregation. For example, teachers may not always want to take Sunday school, but may be happy to provide training.

Reading Groups

Set up a reading group to work through a book about the workplace and faith, perhaps reading a chapter a week or fortnight. Get group members to take it in turns to facilitate discussion about what has been learnt.

Survey

Write a simple questionnaire and ask people to complete it to discover where they work, how many hours, what their greatest challenges and opportunities are, and prayer requests. Act on these, for example by reducing additional demands on those who work long hours.

Part-time Job

Encourage the congregational leader/s to take up a part-time job to experience the marketplace if they haven't been in it for some years. This will mean they have to let a few other things go for a while, but the benefit could be surprising.

Pastoral Visiting

Ask people if you can visit them in their workplace so you can find out more about their working life and how to support them. If that isn't easy, meet for breakfast, lunch or after-work drinks near their workplace.

Cell Groups

Set up some workplace cell groups for people in similar occupations, geographical locations or (if in a smaller congregation) just those in the workplace.

Prayer

Focus prayer on workers as missionaries in the mission field of the workplace. Pray for those at work in all your normal prayer settings such as congregational meetings, prayer meetings and in prayer diaries.

Appendix B

Books

Many books have been written recently about the challenge of integrating work and faith. Below are a few of the best that I am aware of, and a brief summary of each to help you find your way around the library.

In alphabetical order:

Matt Bird with Craig Borlase, *Destiny*. (London, Hodder & Stoughton, 2000) – *Destiny* encourages you to discover and deepen your God-given vocation in life, whatever occupation you might be in. It does this by exploring seven pictures of what it means to be a leader for Jesus Christ within your sphere of influence.

Matt Bird with Craig Borlase, *Manifesto for Life*. (London, Hodder & Stoughton, 2001) – *Manifesto for Life* explores a cocktail of everyday lifestyle challenges and how faith in Jesus Christ is integral to them all. Issues include: identity and image, work and career, friends and family, relationships and sexuality, money and shopping, justice and society, culture and stuff, time and self-management, and church and community.

Matt Bird with Adam Eakins, *The JoshGen Guide to Manifesto for Life*. (London, Joshua Generation, 2002) – This guide is based on the book and offers nine ready-to-use sessions for use in small groups about whole life discipleship.

Marcus Buckingham and Donald O Clifton, *Now, Discover Your Strengths*. (New York, The Free Press, 2001) – This book provides the opportunity to complete The Gallup Organization's personal style inventory called 'Strengths Finder' on the Internet and then helps you understand your unique combination of strengths.

Catholic Bishop's Conference of England and Wales: Committee for the World of Work, *A Spirituality of Work*. (London, Catholic Media Trust, 2001) – 'Work is obviously a human activity, but it can transcend into a divine activity when directed to the glory of God and the good of all humankind.'

Mark Greene, *Christian Life and Work*. (London Bible College, 2000) – This is a small group resource containing a leader's guide, video to be used in the group, and a copy of *Thank God it's Monday*. The six sessions explore some of the key issues people face at work.

Mark Greene, *Supporting Christians at Work: without going insane*. (Sheffield, Administry, 2001) – A booklet for church leaders full of ideas subtitled '90 minutes that could transform your ministry, and your people's.'

Mark Greene, *Thank God it's Monday: Ministry in the workplace*. (Bletchley, Scripture Union, 1997) – Full of good stories and practical wisdom this book aims to help us work for God at work. The second edition takes account of the longer hours of work and the reduction in job security.

Don Latham, *Being Unmistakably Christian at Work.* (Bradford Upon Avon, Terra Nova Publications, 2000) – Don has a unique style and experience that he draws from in this booklet addressing workplace issues.

Don Latham, *Everyday Faith.* (Bradford Upon Avon, Terra Nova Publications, 2001) – Applying Jesus' teaching from the Sermon on the Mount to the workplace.

David Oliver, *Work: Prison or Place of Destiny?* (Milton Keynes, Word, 1999) – Oliver is described in the foreword as 'a passionate man, with a burning desire to give Christians a sense of destiny, purpose and support in the workplace.' This is shown in the book as he helps to correct the opinions that stop us being free to thrive in our workplace.

David Oliver and James Thwaites, *Church That Works.* (Milton Keynes, Word, 2001) – *Church That Works* combines the best of *Work: Prison or Place of Destiny?* and *Church Beyond the Congregation* and then goes further.

Rob Parsons, *Heart of Success.* (London, Hodder & Stoughton, 2002) – The book tells the story of an MBA student who undertakes a personal coaching from a retired professor about making it in business without losing it in life.

Christian Schumacher, *God in Work.* (Oxford, Lion, 1998) – *God in Work* draws on the Christian doctrine of the trinity as a pattern for relationships in the workplace.

R Paul Stevens, *The Abolition of the Laity: Vocation, Work and Ministry in a Biblical Perspective.* (Carlisle, Paternoster, 1999) – Stevens argues theologically that the divide between clergy and laity has no basis in the New Testament and so we are all called to participate in God's mission.

Matt Stuart, *Studentdom: A guide to student life from application to graduation.* (Eastbourne, Kingsway, 2002) – This book is essential reading for any teenager preparing for, or student living in, or graduate moving from, the world called 'Studentdom' which is inhabited by over 5 million people in the UK.

James Thwaites, *The Church Beyond the Congregation.* (Carlisle, Paternoster, 1999) – The challenge is simple but complex: do away with a Platonic dualism, embrace a Hebrew worldview and see the Church growing up through creation through spheres of work and family.

Appendix C

Organisations

Joshua Generation hosted a forum in 2002 for organisations supporting Christians in the workplace. This is a list of those that attended and one or two others.

A Call to Business –
Serving and equipping men and women in business to see change and transformation in the marketplace.
t.   020 7247 0844
e.   admin@acalltobusiness.co.uk
w.   www.acalltobusiness.co.uk

At Work Together (Spring Harvest) –
Aiming to encourage, support and equip Christians at work through a series of national conferences dealing with workplace issues from a biblical viewpoint. Programme includes Bible teaching, major lectures, workshops, worship and networking.
t.   01825 746512
e.   info@springharvest.org
w.   www.springharvest.org/awt

Christians at Work –
Seeking to encourage, support and equip Christian people in the
workplace, for evangelism, visible witness and fellowship, through
affiliated groups and by encouraging individuals, through various
membership and support schemes.
t.   01788 579738
e.   office@christiansatwork.org.uk
w.   www.christiansatwork.org.uk

Full Gospel Business Men's Fellowship International –
Focussing on evangelism, the 150 chapters of the FGBMFI welcome
men from all Christian churches.
t.   01565 632667
e.   fieldoffice@fgbmfi.org.uk
w.   www.fgbmfi.org.uk

Joshua Generation –
Investing in emerging generations of leaders to transform society.
Supporting young people in the transition to university, students
through university and young adults in their workplace.
t.   020 8947 1313
e.   admin@joshgen.org
w.   www.joshgen.org

London Institute for Contemporary Christianity –
Resourcing Christians for whole-life discipleship from the Transition
Project for graduates to resources for CEOs. Through lively research,
training events, Workwise magazine, cyber-resources.
t.   020 7399 9555
e.   mail@licc.org.uk
w.   www.licc.org.uk

International Chamber of Christians in Commerce –
Encouraging and equipping Christians in the market place to come
into a new dimension of faith required for work in these turbulent
times.
t.   0117 924 9754
e.   office@uk.iccc.net
w.   www.uk.iccc.net

Midweek in Mayfair –

Seeking to equip those in the marketplace to be effective disciples for Jesus through preaching and teaching, outreach and pastoral care.

t.   020 7629 2348

e.   chris.dinsdale@midweek.org.uk

Ridley Hall Foundation –

Relating Christian faith to the business world through running residential seminars for businesspeople on topical global, corporate and personal issues and co-publishing the quarterly journal *Faith in Business*.

t.   01223 741074/741082

e.   rah41@cam.ac.uk

w.   www.ridley.cam.ac.uk

WorkNet Partnership –

Helping Christians integrate faith with work by providing week by week support, materials and programmes to connect, equip and resource individuals, groups and churches.

t.   020 8764 8080

e.   info@worknetuk.org

w.   www.worknetuk.org

YWAM Business as Missions Team –

Providing opportunities for Christian business professionals to use their skills beyond their workplace, especially in the least reached and least developed regions of the world.

t.   01582 463244

e.   bam@oval.com

w.   www.ywam-england.com

There are Christian associations for most of the major professions – such as the Christian Police Association. To find out about them why not visit www.christianhandbook.org.uk where for a fee you can download information.

Joshua Generation

Joshua Generation's vision is to develop leaders and influencers in every sector of society to see their lives as integral to the transformation of society whether in family, health, education, law and order, business, media, arts or politics.

The Joshua Generation team work with individuals and groups in workplaces, denominations and networks of congregations, and organisations large and small, facilitating their work and shaping what it means to be the future church. Our approach is to encourage one to one mentoring friendships, offer tailor-made interactive training and offer practical written resources to help people to transform society.

Joshua Generation
The Church
Worple Road
Wimbledon
London
SW19 4JZ

t.   *020 8947 1313*
f.   *020 8947 9414*
e.   *admin@joshgen.org*
w.   *www.joshgen.org*